SAINTS+SINNERS

2025
NEW POETRY
FROM THE FESTIVAL

SAINTS+SINNERS

2025
NEW POETRY
FROM THE FESTIVAL

With an introduction by our judge
Nikki Ummel

Edited by
Jan Edwards Hemming & Paul J. Willis

Saints+Sinners
2025

Published in the United States of America by
REBEL SATORI PRESS
rebelsatori.com

SAINTS+SINNERS
2025 NEW POETRY FROM THE FESTIVAL

ISBN: 978-1-60864-367-7

Credits
Editors: Jan Edwards Hemming and Paul J. Willis
Cover Image by Timothy Cummings
Cover Design by Toan Nguyen
Book Design by Sven Davisson

Contents

Winner, Saints+Sinners Poetry Contest 2025
**Runner-Up, Saints+Sinners Poetry Contest, 2025*

ACKNOWLEDGMENTS

The John Burton Harter Foundation for their continued generous support of the Saints and Sinners LGBTQ+ Literary Festival.

The LGBTQ Fund administered through The Greater New Orleans Foundation.

Timothy Cummings, cover artist for the 2025 Saints+Sinners poetry anthology.

Everyone who has entered the contest and/or attended the Saints+Sinners Literary Festival over the past twenty-two years for their energy, ideas, and dedication in keeping the written word alive in the LGBTQ+ community.

Previous Winners

2024
Holly Zhou

2023
Isobel A. Burke

2022
Michael Montlack

2021
Danielle Bero

Judge's Introduction

Reader, the journey you are about to embark on will change you, reshape you, and perhaps even heal you and make you more whole. Such was my experience reading the poems for this year's Saints+Sinners Poetry Contest, and I am thrilled you get to experience this delectable collection, exactly as you are.

And make no mistake, dear reader—this collection is delectable. It is brimming with poems that highlight the highs and lows, and everything in between, that constitute queer existence (and resistance). It is rich with beauty, wonder, irony, joy, grief, and everything else that makes us human. This leads me to the most important part of this introduction: the reminder that being LGBTQIA+ is to be human. Our humanity is too often scrutinized, minimized, ignored, trampled. It is sometimes alarmingly easy to be swallowed in the rhetoric and forget our own beating hearts. This is where poetry, and specifically queer poetry, rises to guide us, to bring us back to ourselves, to our very human, very queer hearts. Every poet and every poem in this collection has something critical to share with us, to remind us and take our hands and lead us back to a place where we can begin again. How impossible this made selecting a winner and finalists, and how preciously I weighed the gift of each poem submitted. From Jendi Reiter's refreshing celebration of self in "I Hit on My 20-Year-Old Self," where the speaker surrounds their former self with entreaties: "Sugar sugar, I sing," to Branwell Roberts' "Marsyas, flayed by Apollo," with the speaker also finding new voice, "before / my mouth was full - I could not sing. But now I can." And there's Arumandhira Howard, who begins her poem "Chel" with "The mirrors on my island never reflected girls like us," which resonates, across page and space and time with Daniel W.K. Lee's "Indications of a Suicide": "Grief is a bone saw. What limbs will be left to hold on?"

More than anything, this collection is about you. About us. About what makes us, us. A community. The community. Home. You are home, here. There is space for you. Take off your shoes. Stay awhile.

Dearest reader, I am so lucky to be writing this and connecting with you across time and space and existence itself, each of us journeying through our own wild and precious lives. We are so lucky to be here, now. No, seriously. This moment, and this one, and this one, to be alive and queer and to know the full range of being human and to experience that with other members of the LGBTQIA+ community, to laugh and sing and hug and cry and scream and rage, to exist, to resist, to be. here. now. It is magic. You are magic. This collection is magic. So what are we waiting for?

Let's begin.

Nikki Ummel
Judge, 2025 Saints+Sinners Poetry Contest

Editor's Note

In my third year of editing this anthology, I found myself floored by the ways in which the fifteen finalists' poems spoke to one another; even the visual imagery echoed across entries. The work felt more united than ever, despite the fact that this year's contest did not have a set theme.

As I arranged the pieces, I couldn't stop thinking about how these queer folks from all around the globe had created work separately yet still sounded a universal message. Perhaps it happened this way because we all exist as part of a community that many often seek to erase; or because we all inhabit an earth whose future seems so fragile; or simply because we are all writers, beings bound by the urge to compose things that might allow us to live or make sense of living or just outlive us. Or perhaps Jung was right, and this anthology is proof of some really beautiful LGBTQ+ archetype in the collective unconscious.

Whatever the reason for this serendipity, the best way I could think to honor the gift of it was with a poem:

Proof of the Living

What do we have without words?
Without the shape of a self
in ink—an indelible
confirmation of humanity—
we might be buried
by grief, suffocated beneath
the ashes of things both lost
and longed for. You can choke, too,
on a wish, on the vapors of what's past,
on the utter redness of living:
the crackle of a cigarette's cherry, the stain
of a stranger's strawberry lipstick.

The house burns; the body bleeds.
Call it vermillion or scarlet or ruby,
but a scar is a scar is a scar.
We can stay alive if we keep
our eyes open, but they must
be held so, so wide.

And it is hard work, the existing,
the mourning, the putting of pen
to paper. We let our letters
try the impossible: to cut
water with a knife, to scrape
serrated edges of wit and want
and scream, *I am here*—
to etch a future into being—
I am here—
a performance of permanence,
some literary phoenix
who gets to choose, this time,
who they love and how they live.
Before we are fossils in a riverbed,
before the funeral, show me
who you've always been,
and, artist to artist,
I promise to remember you.

Jan Edwards Hemming
Editor, 2025 Saints+Sinners Poetry Contest

Mandy Shunnarah

mx. potato head at the gender swap meet

"On February 25, 2021, Hasbro dropped the honorific in the brand name and began marketing the toy simply as 'Potato Head,' while retaining the individual characters of Mr. and Mrs. Potato Head. However, several media outlets misinterpreted the announcement as stating that all Potato Head products would henceforth be gender neutral." —from the Wikipedia entry on Mr. Potato Head

At the yard sale where no one pays, they come
to dump their cast-offs: the sequined jumpsuits
that jived with gender just once, the fast-fashion
shoes, size 11 (because what drag queen has money
for Manolos & she wouldn't wear them to the sticky-
floored gay club if she did, henny), the 90s
button-downs (all color-block & embroidered
polo players on the breast to worry the raised edges
of top surgery battle scars in the making) &
the zines on brewing bathtub estrogen.

Imagine if we could switch body parts
as easily as clothes, like the Potato Head family:
My mammoth mammaries for your phallus,
ma'am? Your biceps for my muffin top?
Your Adam's apple & jutting jaw for my smooth
cheeks & cavernous pit of pleasure? Instead:
a black derby hat for a plastic pearl necklace,
a stick-on mustache & blue sneakers for a pink pony
purse & purple-lidded falsies—your grandpa-sweatered
cottagecore for my fashion school failout eclectic.

1

& so many handkerchiefs in every color
of the hanky code, you could jump into a pile
like raked leaves & smile for a chosen family
photo to go on the mantel of your childhood home.
Like the school pics & glamor shots you wish you had—
the ones that show who you've always been.

a polycule in the multiverse

Think of us all as a solar system. I could be vain
& imagine myself the sun, but instead, consider me Saturn.

Not its rings—I don't need commitment—but
its fifty-three confirmed moons & the speculative ones, too.

      Endless possibilities from here to negative infinity.

I'm not saying there's fifty-three of us, but that there's enough
to go around. I'm not saying we have orgies, but

a polycule is a chosen family & this much love is luxury.
Yet, if I were forced to choose just one, who would I

say I'm most deeply in love with? If I could only
save one in a fire, who would I pick?

I'm still unlearning, denying myself extravagance since
some think me greedy with feasting & wild revelry,

so I give myself thought experiments to box my affections in—
but I'm asking the wrong questions.

      What if the limit does not exist?

If, in the grand scheme of the cosmos, a multitude of multiverses
allows us each the possibilities that would make monogamy moot?

      Love is not one thing, but many:

infinite untold joy & sorrow & the inarticulable mass between.
What if the question is not whether I am greedy, but whether

it's truly so much to want? I could have a life
with any of them. I could have a life with all of them.

I could be a moon & its planet, too.

picking my switch, or poem in the shape of my lover's hip bone

Cast out from the stone house,
exiled by my mother—hand on
her hip & jaunty knee jutting
from the swaying wood porch—
I entered the holler forest in search
of my switch. Pick a tree limb too thick
& the spank would be a crash that ripened
into a plum-fisted bruise. Too thin & it'd slice like
concertina wire, blooming bloody. As much as I courted
trouble, I became intimate with this in-between, this some
of this, a little of that. I taught myself longing in a compass
of directions & found desire for a plethora of genders.
As soon as my second wrist is tied, I've Houdinied
from the first; the silk rope around their top-
surgeried chest—until they topple me
& my euphoric tower upon their hips.
Genderfluid bisexual Libra, I've been
flirting with decisive straddling, this
liminal middle before I knew its name—
yet this in-between has always known me.

insurance for immortality

after "How will you / have you prepare(d) for your death?" by Chen Chen

buy books faster than you read them   listen to song lyrics like they're horoscopes

    adopt a cat, then another & another   twirl your finger in the hair of your lover

        say i love you without expecting it back   accumulate yarn for arts & crafts

leave a list of sorrys to say   house projects to do   groceries to bring home

write letters you don't finish   & letters you don't send   in licked envelopes

have a drawer full of reading glasses   & another full of twist ties   & one for buttons

      say let's hang out soon & mean it   stack piles of mail unread

    add to the Christmas ornament trove   keep a dozen books on the nightstand

buy toilet paper & canned beans in bulk   make dinner plans as many nights as you can

order a *New Yorker* subscription   & make a promise   to read every feature

stuff plastic grocery bags full   of other plastic bags   & fill a kitchen drawer

collect mugs of pens   & cabinets of figurines   & vases of matches

   & kiss him   & kiss him   & kiss him   & kiss him   & kiss him

    & kiss her   & kiss her   & kiss her   & kiss her

     & kiss them   & kiss them   & kiss them

      to live forever

Daniel W.K. Lee

Runner-Up, Saints+Sinners Poetry Contest 2025

Indications of a Suicide

Sand covers the scarlet traces of a descent. After the police clear the yellow tape, a sedan rolls over the spot that cradles our braided stares.

On the phone, a brother repeats the beginning—*It can't be true. It can't be true*—unsung like the chorus of an unsingable song.

On the phone, an hour later, a sister doesn't know to brace for the anti-gospel: *I'm sorry to have to be the one to tell you this…He's gone.* Just as in Revelations come screams.

He could not wait another day for…

He probably didn't know either.

*

Grief is a bone saw.

I keep writing it in different places like graffiti. I want to carve it somewhere near St. Louis Cathedral, his favorite place, where he told me: were the world different, maybe he would not act like a man.

Grief is a bone saw.

What limbs will be left to hold on?

*

A bootleg heart breaks in so many ways today.

Curb stomped. Incinerated. Dropped. Eroded. I'd say.

Breath, be my witness.

*

You didn't leave a suicide note. Just my phone number in red ink, defiantly perpendicular to the notepad paper's ruling, on the coffee table, where the facilities manager found it. Called me after I already knew. Asked if I was your father.

There is such heft. That shorn-off sheet, heaped with duty, withstood each open window's every inhale.

You knew I could swallow these sad honors: to un-burden those left carrying questions like bouquets, to sweep any wreck(age) in your wake. Even the landslide of your siblings' voices. Even our rubble hearts.

*

An endlessly edited list of things delivers diluvian cheeks: the first cool weather, Rose Betts' "Song to the Siren," the fragrance of an empty passenger seat...

Levees overcome from this relentless gone-ness, this forced amputation.

I become a city with no flood lines inside one with them.

*

You become a bust of other people's wants ground down to dust.

Oh, you beautiful fuckface! is all the fury mustered since. The only complaint requiring no clarity.

*

His voice ricochets down the hollow parts. It's an echo with a phantom source. Tonight, I insist it is the love that persists.

*

Tu familia soaked in shame, shovels silence over your creations: August's adolescence, a Jesus-less altar, bonds beyond bloodline.

They, who know nothing of your reverence to the moon, take turns mugging your memory and clutch victimhood like strands of pearls. What would you have me do about their monopoly over your orphaned novel and powdered marrow?

Against your dad's interdiction, I grafted August (you) to an essay to stave off decay. I won't let winter come so easily.

*

Lips prone to canker sores finally offer a piercing stock of pain. Suffering diversified, at last. It doesn't hurt for you, does it? It doesn't hurt for you.

*

For some, for others, the address is Chernobyl, St. Charles Ave.

Riding the streetcar through, I'll never not look up.

Dementia

What's left of this life happens between blinks.
Often it is the Hudson River, with peels of dusk
mottling the water, that I see from this tomb
of a body. New Jersey spoils an even horizon
but remains the forerunner of my affections.
She will be there to receive me should I return.

A graying woman who calls me "Mom" brandishes
produce: a red Holland bell pepper, tangerines,
Japanese eggplant, shapes sporting every color
of twilight that I suspect is for my benefit.
Yet I never recall eating—or hunger.

When did I become this still? Today, my son
is battered by my un-parted lips, which to him,
stubbornly refuse to speak my mind. If he glimpses
stray tears, he turns away to save his own.
But if he wouldn't, he'd hear what they've been saying
for so, so long: "It's time. And it's okay."

Lauren Howton

On the Bank of the Wakulla River

stick your feet on in for a redneck pedicure
and watch the boats trawling tour groups
back and forth   the occasional ripples
scare the minnows at your feet
but they will come right back to you
too small to understand your abundance

let's let the river make of us a buffet
take all the skin we're trying to slough off

down at the bottom of the spring
there are mastodon bones and catfish
six-foot-long giants that used to be visible
until the water got murked with fertilizer
that drained into the spring with the runoff

those bones used to rise and fall
like the tide over lungs bigger than you
when we were just spits of water somewhere
and gators with scarred up scoots lay by
dreaming of dusk and cooter sandwiches

there's a ranger on the front of a pontoon
holding a guitar singing about anhingas
and pied-billed grebes   he's not great
but he's good   so good like this greenness
we're going to help each other clear the water

eventually I'll be okay with watching

the minnows get eaten by the birds
and those river angels eaten by the alligators
everything is moving so fast on the Wakulla
it's down to the ocean already and still

the soft moss finds time to chain it all down
starting with what's left of my toes

Lambent Endings

it's hard to know when to leave the fireside
when embers only light our shins or before
when there's still flame pinking our cheeks
when the dog's given up trying to find a way
to his friends on the other side of the fence
they bark *don't leave us* and *come back please*
we stood out here under so many full moons
until cloud cover sent us back inside to bed
sometimes we talked so long our faces hurt
I don't care what you say   we were mesmerized
not by the flame but by something absent
glass taking on vermillion hues before it cools
so many earthworms uprooted themselves
when we took the bricks up barehanded
scraping our knuckles bloody   before the house
was sold so many rusted bottle caps fell hidden
between cracks the grass will grow thick in spring
fed by the charcoal left behind you knew though
when to plant the bricks on an early autumn night
Florida puts winter on like a swatch of bad paint
in a bare living room things go back to normal
and only worms will be left wanting old shelters

Morphology

there was an empty flower pot
on the front porch through winter
a little vacancy from the mother
of thousands I killed last year
the beautiful woman at the nursery
told me I'd know it was healthy
when it filled its margins
with plantlets
they looked parasitic
all those children attached
to the leaf
my problem was I left
it outside after a breakup
we got a freeze and she turned
I took that withered husk
to the compost abandoned
the pot knowing I couldn't make
anything else grow there
plant nor pot should count on me
today I noticed a brown orb
of nest filling the terracotta
like some earthen snow cone
inside sat a perfect celadon egg
something I didn't want to touch

Getting Undressed

it was so simple the way she said
excuse me but your dress looks like this
she shows me a Matisse painting
and everything is now wallpapered
red my dress on the ceiling my dress
on the table and under our purses
this woman must carry the whole history
of art behind her eyelids must summon
sunflowers in a bare room great waves
in droughts when she's empty-bellied
she calls baskets of Caravaggio's fruit
I'm in the room covered by myself
the red is monstrous I want to love it
but there's no place to hide from it
the dress is now up around our faces
like Magritte's *Lovers* if we speak
any more we may choke on the fabric

Branwell Roberts
Runner-Up, Saints+Sinners Poetry Contest 2025

Catullus 63

You could hardly have been the flower
of the gymnasium, grappling, oiled, in rippling
boy-body, not the way you look—
so soft and tender, pretty little fraud.
Instead you dance and clap and stamp your feet,
and sing soprano with the forest's girls.
They run with the hunt, every day faster
and further off into the ready-made future
into which someone like you can never follow.
Someday you'll be discovered—they will tear
after you, chasing with wild beasts at their heels.
But dance for now, Leucippus, dance and play
your tambourine. They'll rip deeper than skin
to find you out. You were almost a girl.

The Epicene

Next to the wooden barrier studded with barnacles,
great chunks and planks of it torn out by the tide,
I crouched low where the sea wall met the beach.

With the handle of my fishing net I scratched
an image into wet sand; first a bearded face,
a hairy chest but then completed with

a child's idea of breasts—two circles and two dots.
A magician working a magic circle,
I moved the stick around me, etching arms, legs,
then stalling when I reached the middle part.

The tide was getting high and I retreated,
panicked, through the seaweed-dripped divide.
The sea swallowed the furtive, scuffed-out picture
and held it in its mouth, to be conjured again.

Marsyas, Flayed by Apollo

Strung up by my feet for my bad music,
my lower pelt now hangs in tatters round
my head, like a girl's skirt flying in the wind.
Below my hips is smooth and red with blood.

The kissing knife that licks me into shape
is pushed under the tongues of pulled-back hide,
and saws the flesh there so that the proud god
can tear it off and ease me from myself.

He is exact, severs my skin in one
clean piece with that never-wandering eye
you find only in huntresses or surgeons.
I see now he has always had my measure.

Soon my arms will be sliced into red opera gloves:
denuded, quivering under steady hands.
A stranger light shines through me now, before
my mouth was full—I could not sing. But now I can.

Arumandhira Howard

Runner-Up, Saints+Sinners Poetry Contest 2025

Chel

The mirrors on my island never reflected girls like us. So I sat
with my chin tipped towards the black box you lived inside.
The bend of your waist. Lunar bow linking blood cells into a wire
you loop around my neck and reel. I was five and ready to stand
in a rain of arrows for you. Prepared to lather myself in the
    quicksand
of your brown arms. Grandmother called you a bad woman for
showing your wrists, your ankles, your dimpled back—to which
I returned a funeral smile. You wouldn't be the last woman to toss
her hair at my frothed offering. Chel. You're the reason. Now I look
for me in every woman I dare to open. Spines stoned by men
we idoled into gods. You gargled Tulio's lie like peppercorn.
You had to make him believe, for a second, he was worthy
of your worship. Like how Auntie apologized to Uncle
for the plums he planted across her desert. Before him,
she was in magazines. He moved through the Japanese
underworld with a katana and Soviet pistol. Neither were
enough for him. So she forced herself shapeless in a black cloak
to assure him she was his planet to annex. *This*, Grandmother
considered to be the decor of a *weak* woman. *Your aunt looks like
a ninja but she can't fight back.* Auntie's eyes fought to prove
existence from behind a lunette of mesh. Tell me, Chel,
are all beautiful born into ritual sacrifice?
There will always be a master, a man, a maker who wants
more than what they deserve. You found none of this foreign.
How to wield a white lie to anchor sight without being claimed.
Pleating your legs, tucking them fetal. Vertebrae, contoured into
harmless architecture. So they could lick their lips from

afar. So they saw you as a monument, too exquisite
to demolish.

Between Floors

If we fell thirteen stories, our bodies propelling like pinballs, the law of physics exploding our humanity—know it was a perfect day. Summered lawn where they filmed that insufferable romcom. She made me love a splintered bench and this impatient city that never stops gutting. Glass, steel limbs. Claw machines toasting another towering coffin. While prematurely clinking our death in plastic flutes, she disarmed the security guard's threat. Simply smiled like a daughter he missed. She wanted to show me. Cherries and cheese and cured meat was a meal to be enjoyed on a roof. Called it   girl dinner.

[----The elevator hitched like my focus in the air we split----]

▼

Here is a melodramatic trope: queer catastrophe. They (the simulators and idiots with nothing better to do) would not stop killing us for their amusement. I memorized the shape of her nails as she picked a thread on her jeans. How devastatingly ordinary my name sounded leaving her throat, even with death flirting. We stood close in the firemen's hands waiting to be saved but maybe this was the only proper way to suspend a moment in time. *Is this the worst date you've ever been on?* I acknowledged what competed under the pulsing orange of this cramped comet on a string. How my history of wringing the delicate from rot could be comfortable here. But we survived. Jumped into sweated and smoked arms. We promised to spoil this new lease on life with the most expensive girl dinners. Until it just ended. When I left the city (she stayed), the moment punctured through everything. An elevator shaft too deep to pull out of. I couldn't stop going back to it. To her, picking at something I refused to look in the eye. In the box I kept her in, she washed her ginger hair with cardamom, a lover of damp coats on the mattress.

[Trying to answer what I never asked]

Gua Sha as a Window

On my back, Mother cracks
a map of freeways. Rubies,
culled from wineblood.
That's the djinn, she presses
the coin, drilling to exhume
her daughter from under the queer.

In a way, love and pain
are comrades.

Both parasitic,
reliant on a host.
Both revealing.

I am yours in a hymn
Mother can't hum.
You are somewhere
in Vienna, where clouds
feed on skylines.
You never call me back.

We made a deal with death
the day we met just to forget
we're both alive. Forget this.

Hours collapse like cards between
breastbone. We sleep in a world
that has never stopped ending.

Still digging, Mother engraves
a pair of violet wings,
but I can't fly. I am hers
in a tongueless hymn.

So I play you on a loop
like a happy glitch.
You, coated in television
glow. You, ears to the dirt,
telephoning our next life.

Where catmint spoons
cantaloupe sky and God
is the moan charioting
your breath to mine.

You're here with me,
I'm there with you—inside you.
And inside me, you are some sort
of window, crescent with dancing
twilight.

I leave it ajar.

I (28F) Am Just a Girl. AMA

What is it like holding the reins?
Conditional keys. Pre-approved route.
Tires skidding into a weed-flowered
ditch. Don't push the pedal too hard.

Do you know how to bloom?
Strawberry Fanta fizz. Sticky aftermath.
Lick the stick off, then get all red.
You're not supposed to finish.

Is your spirit swole?
Bath bombs, Etsy rock, ASMR. Aqua Stanley
while oceans dehydrate. Go nap in a plush peach
sleep mask and bliss it off.

How do you know it's love?
Semi-colon smoke rings. White charger
haunting your closet. Collapsing into a black hole,
white hole, yellow hole. The stars don't give a fuck.

When will it be worth it?
When it hits you right. Right hippo meme
that makes you pee, right amount of pepperoni grease,
right hand down a pair of jeans, right wrist

righting you, trying to rage quit.

Joshua Kulseth

Fourteen Rounds of Looking at Joe Frazier

Manila, October 1975

I.

Is Joe Frazier
a white champion
in black skin?

In Beaufort he moves
to cash his winnings. The eyes
of the teller look down
to the massive black hands
holding the check,
look up. The white head shakes,
draws a pointed finger
to the door.

The Heavyweight Champion of the World:
Joe Frazier.

II.

Body. Head. Body.
He sweats and aches.

The heavy bag
collects the enormous hands
of Joe Frazier.

III.

Ali:

He works for the enemy.

Turn coat.

Uncle Tom.

Joe Frazier.

IV.

Frazier:

God will mock you down.

He doesn't mock,
he works. The heavy bag
kept swaying
day and night,

the work of Joe Frazier.

V.

Ali:

It's gonna be a killa,
and a thrilla, and a
chilla, when I get
that Gorilla in manilla.

The toy gorilla he fondles

in his massive hands
has the face of a gorilla.

He boxes the face of the gorilla
like he boxes Joe Frazier.

VI.

Frazier:

Why he wanna call me a gorilla
I ain't no gorilla;
I don't look like one—

He's handsome, and serious,
with a nose broken
over and over. Serious
man. Serious
Joe Frazier.

VII.

Joe Frazier watches the television,
watches himself watch
Ali across the ring. Watches
the face of the man
asking him questions.

Chuckles.

He payin' the eternal price now.

VIII.

How he slices the thick jaw,
heaves the body deep,

weaves the thread of his head
under blows,

thick in the groove
he moves,

Smokin' Joe Frazier.

IX.

Ali:

Flat nosed ugly pug.

He don't write no poetry.

Quick thrust of fist.
Knuckled blows:
The poetry of Joe Frazier.

X.

He shrugs and spasms under punches.
Sweats and smiles.
Offers a tap
with gloved fist against
the ass of Ali.

Fourteen rounds.

He slows and staggers,
leans heavy in,
hands down.
The red gloves of Ali
becoming the ears
of Joe Frazier.

XI.

Time is out of joint.
The men waver as if struck
by the heat of fever.

The earth revolves
around Joe Frazier.

XII.

Ali:

That's the closest thing to death
I ever known.

Finish it,

put out his lights, Joe Frazier.

XIII.

The white towel like a dove
wings the brief air,
falls.

The white dove of Joe Frazier.

XIV.

Ali:

He's tough. I'm so tired
I don't wanna do nothin'
for a whole week.

If God ever calls me
to a Holy War
I want Joe Frazier
by my side.

Frazier:

you tell him
I want a rematch.

The waste of his eyes
shine under lights, shine
in flashbulbs, shine
years after, looking back
on the television glow of it all,

looking at Joe Frazier.

Victoria Sosa

I'm Sorry for Being Dramatic

My best party trick is falling gracefully
    like the pale and suffocating women who came before me—
    but my ancestors were the ones pulling their strings,
    hovering in corners with fans and buckets of ice
    to mother and wife and breathe and die in their mistresses' places.
    My mother always accused me of having a white woman inside me.
    Of oppressing her.
    This is to say I was born with the entitlement needed for fainting.
I start by swooning,
a leaf-like sway onto my knees.
I crumble quickly, collapsing my torso, finishing
with my face kissing the floor.
The trick is the soft thud that gives the illusion of pain.
They applaud my performance
but they won't help me off the floor so
that's where you find me.

I've been holding your hand since we first
laced fingers in the cemetery.
You asked if this could be enough.
I said: No.
I want to wake up next to you,
watch you make breakfast in a yellow kitchen,
do the dishes while you cook,
listen to your music on a long drive,
hold you in the backseat when your car breaks down
on the corner of Clouet and Dauphine,
hold you while you cry,
hold you while I cry.
I think our love is going nowhere.

Our love is driving until it's tired, parking where it can't be seen:
walking into the city, the swamps, the mountains—
into the wild.
Our love is making a home underneath the lights just
for itself, just for the night.
Our love doesn't rest but it rises
to walk back to the car and decide on a different direction.

This isn't your love poem. When
I write your love poem
I won't say I fantasize about breaking up with you, walking
away from you, leaving you, disappearing.
Almost as much as I fantasize about you coming home to me.
I'm always naked when you come home to me
or I was just naked
or I'm about to be.

I want to sit you down most nights, explain
how you'd be freer without me until you
agree
and slam my door on your way out,
not because you're angry but
because that's the only way to close my front door.

There are things I'm not saying now.
I learned what's said in this house, stays in this house.
I've traded walls for a rib cage,
which doesn't keep out the cold or keep in my secrets
but at least my heart has a place to rest.
Keep your heart in your own hands,
they've got a better grip than mine.
I realize as you grab my hands
and lift me up

I'm remembering it all wrong.
I told you: Yes,
this could be enough.

The Four Seasons of New Orleans

New Orleans,
I don't know you,
so if you choose not to believe me when
I say, "I love you,"
I understand.
Another pathological liar,
another residential poet
another transplant putting distance between
themselves and their emotions.
Using you to put distance between myself
and the ocean
but still dipping my toes into Lake
Pontchartrain,
still drinking cognac on Bourbon
and hurting strangers desperate to know you.
I pretend I am you.
They want to fuck this city.
Take it as a compliment, New Orleans—
they still think you're pretty.

New Orleans,
I'm untrusting of you
but not in the way most people are.
When things are good
they're really good.
When things are bad
they're pulling up dead bodies on Poets St.,
now St. Roch Ave.,
buying hurricane-proof window pane art.
I'm wearing a shirt that isn't my shirt,
walking in shoes that aren't my shoes,
losing things that aren't mine to lose,
except the things that became mine
because I didn't give them back.
You take things from people
and you don't give them back.
You don't let them go.
I don't let things go;
still, things are pretty good.

New Orleans,
I rented an apartment of yours Uptown
that reminds me of myself,
its dreamy exterior enough to make anyone
stop and stare—
desire, perhaps.
Its interior shows potential
which is realtor talk for:
It has fallen apart.
It has been waiting for someone to care.
I got it for its two closets:
one has a door and one doesn't.
I spent a lot of time deciding
what deserves to be seen.
I wanted to love someone
in the holes of your streets.
If you don't believe in me, New Orleans,
I understand that, too.

New Orleans,
remember when you had no lovers,
only slaves, only red-ribboned whores.
Remember when we had each other.
Invincible, invisible,
we were better strangers than friends.
Forget promises made in our honeymoon
phase. It's easy to promise forever
on a sinking ship
of black and blue skins.
God keeps trying to give me another
shot, push me past my limit.
I don't like mezcal or meditation
or visiting my mother hungover
on Sunday evenings.
New Orleans, I'm leaving,
though angels have fallen from heaven
and for that sin are damned.

Fingers of Rain

You can't do everything on your own.
You can't remove the bones in your left hand
after removing the bones in your right hand
and having no hands won't stop your suffering.
It only makes responding impossible
when they ask the mute woman:
How are things going?

It comes and goes
but mostly it comes and I go
into the sun to hide my face
wearing nothing but a purple raincoat.
It's new, it's got inside pockets
and a vinyl lining that caresses my bare stomach.
The wrong side of my sunglasses are wet—
a precipitated thought—
Dancing
My fingerprints on anyone I've ever loved
The infinite uses of my tongue
The single purpose of my teeth
The sudden realness of my body when it makes contact
Astro traveling back to earth through touch
Faces gather into rain clouds.
I get ready for a baptism in grief.

Tell her anything that happens is just a thing that happened
but let it make her cry.
Crying *I Am Here*
let it make her laugh.

Laughing *I Am Here*
let it make her die
if dying makes things clear.

A piece of a person is still a person.

The two kinds of pain are two cities away
and you travel between them on the public train
where the man across from you pulls out a travel pack of tissues
so you can dry your eyes.
He smiles at you before he gets off
and later when you think of throwing your body on the rocks,
you also think of white Kleenex—
the pure kindness of strangers.
You're still crying
but you don't jump.

Kit Evans

Colors of My Boyhood

red

My fingers blister when I smoke cigarettes down to their filters. Cherry red burnings, climbing into me.

I still peel dried and dead skin off my cracked lips, as if it'll change anything. As if I can rid myself of what's mine.

Blood from my torn mouth—the only lipstick I've ever worn—blots, stains filters red.

And my father still smokes with me on this darkened porch, his own hammer-hard hands scorched.

Through the red, I ask him if he's ever noticed my hands, how they mirror his own.

Singed peach fuzz on the knuckles, new blisters building on the old. Ask if he's noticed how alike we are.

But he speaks of my mother. How red her lips. The cherry bright stain she'd leave on every cigarette.

The Day After Trying to Hang Yourself

we get outta town and drive the coast.
Burst blood vessels in the bags of your eyes,
a petechiae of stars. I buy you salmon
and we tear it up in the car with our fingers,
the windows down, and it all smells like rain and fish.
When the sun sets we roll 'em up, hotbox the car,
crank your noise loud. The only way we can stand it.
Crank it 'til we feel the guitar and bass and slamming drums
in our chests like heartbeats, like the music lives in us,
like we're alive, like you still have a place to live,
like before your dad found out you're gay.
You can't keep your eyes off the ink black waves.
You say everything looks better in the dark,
like stars. But I think the white moths flying
around the streetlight glow like phosphorescence
between the shivering smoke.

Against Dying

I've spent so much time
beating against my own body the
echoes are still bouncing
between my ears every night.
I died in my dreams every night.
I woke just as the bullet struck
my skull. This body that shouldn't have
been mine to begin with heals chipped
and crooked but it's still
mine. I still want to slice these globes
of fatty flesh off my chest in the shower.
I've shattered and mended so many times
I don't remember the absence of ache, but
maybe I like swerving my car towards
every imposing ponderosa pine and busting
my bones on the boulders of the Deschutes
River and feeling the scream of my femur
with each step, but now piles of off-yellow
pills and the unexpected moments
of peaceful silence make my stomach churn.
But what can I do? I've never made
a promise to stay intact. A one-eyed rabbit
thumps its foot against the earth, beating
to the rhythm of *I am still here, I am still here*.

Lungfish

The river cradles a crescent moon,
current smearing slivered light.
My partner asks: *Do you still feel it?*
I know what he's really asking—
does the water in my skin still pull me
barefoot into silt, sand? Do my lungs
still float and air still choke, caught
between tongue, throat?
Do I still wade up to my neck,
the memory of my fetal gills?
Here in the grass and gravel, skin-to-skin,
folded in the dry, I tell him about Dipnoi.
Double-breathers. The lungfish
of Africa and South America
that glaze themselves in mucus,
burrow in mud and wait
through the crack-dry season
for flooding rain. Deep water dreaming.
Something splashes the surface of the river,
a bug-hungry fish, or maybe a mink
diving into midnight. I wonder out loud
where it's going.
Why not follow it? he whispers
in the undercurrent.

Bleah Patterson

A poem about the people who left the family and only came back for her funeral

I missed you   so much that I   / didn't even ask to where you'd been
taken, but you said / no, no   you'd escaped, and I   missed you /
so much I didn't think   to ask you   why you left, who   / had swifted
you away   under the cover of a dew damp, unwashed / blueberry of
a pre-dawn,   and you said no no,   / no one, it was just you. And
when I asked/ if you were staying this time   you said, already out
the window, that /   you're the mimosa tree, been there since before
either of us were even thoughts in our mamas' / heads, all puffed and
pink, swarming   a forgotten thing / until you're   remembered and
we remember everything else too   / all at once

I don't know if I've ever been in love or if I just love the beginning and end of something

as a little girl
I'm made of a larvae   I can't stop squirming
can't stop   begging to be picked up
only to beg to be put down   beg you to
pop me in your mouth   now swallow
don't savor   always gorging myself
I feast on 'once' and   'upon'
plead to skip to 'ever' and   'after' and again
and again   no, I've never been good
at shouldering   the calm, sweet center
of anything   shoveling a grave first
showing up to the date
second   and I always thought
that impatient   crumb of me   might
evolve   larvae to blood-sucking   mosquito
someone who latches on who
won't leave without a thwack
but oh I'm still   just a squirming thing

I can't tell if the noise outside of my bedroom window is the building's fire alarm or cicadas

and like January
     every Texas   May has toddled
   bowlegged   no memory of   summers before
    or of every   wish placed upon it
filled with intentions   condensation
        oozing   off its   forehead
   promising to do better   this time
cracking its own   cavity in half, offering
    between thumb and pointer
  'here have some'   every emptying more holy
than the last   the sun sets   so much later
     rises   so much earlier
forgets   so quickly, it's winter   resolutions
    remembers only   love love
    this year is for love   it must search
follow the scent of   petunias, of   vanilla bean
   of that sweet rotting   morning breath concealed only
in a kiss that promises love   love   cracked in half
  'here have some'   to slurp it down, satiated until
December, until   it forgets until it   remembers

double, quadruple, and whatever comes next—texting my friends until I feel something again

as if   being a fountain
        of unrequited   need
is something   to brag about
        at thirteen   I make a bucket list
                with the girl who's not allowed
to love me back   I   write
6.) love someone who will never love me back
                                as if   that's not
obvious
                        as if we're only   thirteen and
that's what every   thirteen-year-old girl wants
        after reading   her first Nicholas Sparks novel
  because   let's be honest   that is
what every   thirteen-year-old girl wants
        after reading   her first Nicholas Sparks novel
        and people keep asking about
  the worm   as I wriggle around them   all grotted
                viscous want   and I ask them
if they'd love me   *even if*   and some of them
                get it   but most of them   don't

Ash Helms-Tippit

this is where

i tried smoking
behind the building
where i gave
my first blow job
up the hill
from where i
first kissed a girl
down the road
from my first wreck
near where they made
the best muffins
by where i got a tattoo
with a tuba
player from my
hometown
in the field
where my dad and i
found the dragon
under the bridge
where i spent my rent
on art
that got rained on
this place of magic
steel and smashed
ginkgo buds
is where i lived
before it became
where i was from

she was clever

i was frizzed out at midnight
making beer with the boys
and other girls' hair

all that time turning into
helping him study
and hemming my skirt

it wouldn't be such a trick
if i'd looked closer
but i was exactly what i wanted

scared for you
performing pink
or was it blue

did it ever really matter
until the very end
when she was a mirror

and i
a broken reflection

conversation

conversation is a ~~cake. cycle.~~ demand for energy and resources. demanding a beginning that does not end.

when you talked over me—if you wanted conversation—you wouldn't.

you wouldn't.

they say to start with i feel.

i feel. i feel. you know how when someone pulls a gun and they zoom up really close on the eyes. the forehead widens with the sweat glossing over it. when you deadname my wife i see the attempt to crush her scull against pavement. becoming just another headline. blue hair stained red by gritty street. my lungs not expanding enough to make you listen. i feel. i feel. my body retch with the suck of your teeth. just praying to god we survive the conversation.

you've always been

the girl who called me a writer
in the letter in the book you gave me

the year we held hands
in red plastic chairs

above swirling colors
back before we cracked pecans

with my mom who is yours now
the way your mother is to me

i didn't know
too much tuna could cause mercury poisoning

until you told me
and told me i'd be okay

i know these cypress nuts
are hurting us

but i need this bayou bullshit
so here we are

my teeth stuffed with gratitude
and chicory

you take my hand anyway
showing me

a me i couldn't see
before you

and the letter i write back
is addressed to our home

Jendi Reiter

Winner, Saints+Sinners Poetry Contest 2025

I Hit on My 20-Year-Old Self

Baby, I entreat her, this is your moment. You'll never have bigger
hair or smaller feet. Boys your age have dirty socks for brains.
Don't blame yourself for the way they look right through you like a
peephole. You're a black whip on pink leather. You're a basket of the
apples of knowledge. Most men aren't ready for exile, but I am. I was
born where you are, on the wrong side of the bridge.

She walks out of my arm around her, but politely, hunching her
shoulders. Despair is ripe on her like the scent of plums. I'm one of
the absurdities of life that offends her. Another short bald guy the
age of her absent father. They attach themselves to her like a milking
machine.

Darling, I try again, more homosexually. A time will come when the
gods of intoxication call you brother. You will find the right necks
to step on. Meanwhile, try to forgive us for dreaming of plunging
our faces into your hot fountain. After it becomes safe for you too to
surrender down to the root, you'll understand how the gift burns to
be shared.

She says, Stop touching my imagination. It's the sole place I rule. I
liked it better when I was invisible, like the person who turns on the
lights in a house on the hill that you drive past at night. If I'm so
beautiful, why don't I feel real?

Sugar, sugar, I sing. You are my candy deadname. Imagine Betty
kissing Veronica. You don't have to be in this picture. End the teen
movie before the makeover. Splice in the scene where Puck stands

naked at the window of the boys' school, wreathed in the impossible brevity of desire. You took the suicide gun from his hand and fired it into the future. You hit the target you couldn't see. It was my heart. I'll be waiting.

The Worst-Case Scenario Survival Guide: Bisexuality

~How to Avoid Being Struck by Lightning~

Avoid unprotected gazebos. The rainfall will make her skirts heavy as silence. Study the fir trees rather than her eyelashes. Their fringes quiver the same. Count the number of seconds until thunder is heard and multiply by five. This will indicate how far her heartbeat is from yours in miles. In husband's hoofbeats. Keep your heads low as sodden peonies. Current traveling through the ground may use you to bridge the depression.

~How to Catch Fish Without a Rod~

Remove your shirt or undershirt. Scars in the strobe will flicker at him like almost-indifferent smiles. Slip the branch into the place where pain is expected. Mouths opening breathe music thicker than air. Fish usually congregate in shadows like a choir. When your ends are tied together, whatever fills him feels real enough.

~How to Survive Adrift at Sea~

Put on clothes if possible. Tears can damage your skin, lesioning her name on the future you claim to offer unblemished. In a marital emergency, the rule of thumb is that you should step up. You should be up to your waist in water before you point out that her pillow has floated away. Throw your promises overboard. Seaweed will form, wet and knotty as the hair you tried to stroke but pulled instead. Do not exhaust yourself—you will not be able to move any significant distance without great effort.

~How to Escape from a Bear~

Talk loudly, clap, sing, or call out. There'll always be one to chase you into an alley. Who can't resist human food. Pretend you don't hear his leathers and hot breath, insistent as the sea thumping the pier. If he paws your mouth, you won't be able to tell him what he knows: the further, the better. Whatever you do, be heard.

~*How to Win a Bar Fight*~

Attack the most sensitive areas of your lover: kinks, mothers, dreams. Some common objects that can be used as weapons are tongues and mornings. You must be in a pure position. Nutting may allow you to get away.

Help! I've Been Invited to a Cuddle Party

lately since becoming a dickless
man I feel power
over women ignoring
they see me in my Jerry-Orbach-
in-*Dirty-Dancing* golf shirt
as their fathers   in other words
they'll fuck me and be angry
what great confessional
poetry I'm seeding
in this neck massage

a weedy warmth
I smell the roots of her hair
is this sex
to be open to disgust
he picks up my foot
like it's his own
taint he's pressuring with his thumb
I regret my argyle socks

is this sex when a baby
becomes a porcupine
so his mother's waves of hungry love
don't crawl all the way inside
my first memory
is holding my breath
Patrick Swayze is dead

but this man sweats like him
stretching his ropy dancer's arms
across my chest my nice
flat itchy scars
I could do something

to this woman's stomach I want to touch
like a water bed
to that man who intimidates me like a horse
is this sex when I lie
crushing his hard hipbones
he rolls his proud eyes
I sink into my own gut like Baby
when the mean girls in daffodil-cup dresses
whisper about her back-kitchen tango

I apologize for leaning on his windpipe
I am not losing my hair in a fashionable way

at home my husband has a broken leg
is this sex when I hold the bowl
for his mouthwash spit
and kiss his unplastered toe while we watch Errol Flynn
leap gallantly from the galleon's rigging
my husband does not want to cuddle Errol Flynn
I used to want him to fuck me but now I just want his boots

is this sex when as a galley slave
he's whipped filthy and shirtless
I felt at age ten I shouldn't have seen that
hot and disturbed if I wasn't
pure something would kill me
that was when I became a pervert
I invited my husband to the cuddle party
in his wheelchair but he squeaked
like *The Sea Hawk*'s Spanish maiden
when the rose thorn pierces her thumb

his movie is over
the queen has declared victory
and I wash his balls with a sponge

Daniel Meltz

Outstanding Performance by an Actor in a Supporting Role

She lights cigarettes from cigarettes and can never bundle warm
    enough. He has
Chevron stripes across both delts and a wiseguy smile. The daughter
    likes to
squeeze the son with possessive headlocks. The grandmother likes to
    jab herself in
the rolled-down thigh as seagulls angle out the window, high
    overhead, in isopropyl

martyrdom. She's as scrawny as a scallion but they call her Big
    Freida. There are
children in the dirt and hiding under buildings. There are children in
    the evening till
the moon comes out. There are ice cream sellers in white with
    bowties pulling on
silver sundown latches with a heartbroken suck on the seal. There's
    the squash of

adjoining cardboard apartments on a dandelion corner near a
    supermarket where
groceries roll out on conveyor belts. And the outdoor movie with its
    dialog wafting
over a black steamy night, a plinking river. Romantic patter. Psychotic
    screaming.
The solution of a morning when there's nothing to adjust to. The
    solution of a

teacher who is sexy with second graders but not in the way you think.

The other
teacher, the man teacher, who betrays them with his manly powers
    but who makes
them want to relinquish their lives, anything to be with him, while
    somehow getting
rid of his wife and kid. There's the night they know they love each
    other, Pete

and Noreen, at the Peppermint Lounge. And Gray, right after his
    father dies, alone
at that bar where the Samuel Beckett look-alikes go, punching out a
    stranger. And
Macaroni Bob with his elbow on a mantelpiece, eyes almost crossed
    with thoughts
of his grand ambitions. Lost loves of exemplary character: a dynamo,
    a Romeo, a

Harlequin, a conqueror. The languages they speak! The half-finished
    joints they
pick up off the concrete floors after open-air concerts! The
    kaleidoscopic hard-ons!
The opportunities for self-pitying sobbing—thrilling neurotic
    interludes accompanied
by Rachmaninoff—and the disappointments too fresh to be
    understood. Oh

the guys you might follow around through the streets of the Far West
    Village like
a detective with only a courtroom artist's sketch to go on, brothers of
    the unrequited
crushes that amount to a single archetypal crush—a lot of people are
    him—you
know what that feels like, don't you? And the friends you can count
    on to get

desperately trashed with and dance with or hug like dipsos in a

cinnamon-tinted
Dipso movie, same friends since you first got started. Elizabeth
    Bishop, Eartha Kitt,
Henry James, Patricia Hitchcock. The widow who lives with her
    hard-ass mother
for sixty-eight years in a mannish hat and coat like the hat and coat
    of the psychiatric matron

in *A Streetcar Named Desire*. The ecstasy dealer whose wife leaves him
    flat so he never
bothers to love again and remarries a farina-white seamstress with
    dominatrix lipstick.
Plus of course his whimsical nephew. And you—you!—with your two
    thousand thread
count Palermos of love and nowhere else to go or hide because I'm
    futures in your history.

Before Your Membership Expires

Once upon a time I was a basket-case pothead—all I had was my
flushed-away youth—yet I honored a subpoena to the court of
romantic stand-off, copping to a crush on a dangerous hero, lying

under oath that I didn't want to change him—that I didn't want
to sweet-talk him into hanging up the stun gun and telling me he
loved me—as I swore on a stack of Emerson's essays in the quaverless

voice of the suddenly consequential (something I never imagined
I'd be) that I was sure I understood my love-doctored destiny. I took
the stand every couple of months (serial offender; too much tequila)

until many years later when I cornered Mr. Bigstuff at a speed
dating event. And what once was a worry as combustible as a wish-
bone in a wildfire (would I ever find love with a sensible guy?)

was suddenly a theater date and a strip-club date and a recipe for
no-knead bread and getaway plans on Hotels-dot-com, whispering
discount codes to my own true love. And of course there were con-

flicts (beach vs. mountains, your get-up-and-go vs. my couch-potato
ass, the shock of a hollering neighbor vs. the banging on the ceiling)
but I reported to you in full, an underqualified diplomat, trailing my

tacky history of bullshit promises, heartless gossip, lies about
things that didn't matter and gratuitous attacks on workplace
colleagues because, well, come on, they asked for it—but who had

also sought truth beyond a virtueless world of curdled compliments
and preening selfies—and is zeroing in on the point of his suspense.
Not death, no, but what our lives will be like beyond this year's

elections. Because it's only you and I these days, after dinner in front

of the sunset window, under generous stained-glass living room
lampshades, triumphing over self-disapproval, debating what's okay

for us to joke about and what's off limits, toying with public nudity
and innocent brutality and cactus kisses and tone of voice. As I act
the part of human antenna with my right hand paralyzed on the
    edge

of the cactus windowsill. As I touch-type sestinas and unrhymed
sonnets on the subject of your chin (a lot like the head of your
penis) into this thirteen-year-old Chromebook laptop and

ponder your inability to boast or exaggerate or cross a line that I
thoughtlessly crossed again and again until the line disappeared.
And here we are winners of the great homosexual sweepstakes.

John Costello of the Revolution

He towered over the customers—the ones who'd come for poems and
    the ones
who'd come for beer—as he was taller than a subway door and as
    meaty as a
Saharan bull or a stuntman in a football movie. I sat at a stool when
    the reading

was over and ordered a Guinness and looked for him, though it
    seemed he'd left
so why had I bothered; then he sat down beside me and affably,
    generously
made conversation. I juddered like a flat-stemmed leaf. (I'd planned
    to recite my

poems and go—I was last in the lineup—but I'd seen him before the
    other reciters
had even shown up, and his bigness put a dent in me. He had to've
    noticed my
gawking at him.) I was stunned that he sat with me and said he
    enjoyed my poem

about a friend who'd double-crossed me. I'd assumed he was one of
    the put-
upon locals obliged to keep their voices down while haughty
    Manhattanites
hijacked their refuge with windy cadence and pompous blather. He
    said, "Pretty

exploosive, pretty pissed off," with some kind of burr at the top of his
    voice. I
learned that his game was soccer, not football, that he captained a
    team
in Van Cortlandt Park, lived in Queens with a couple of roommates,

was born

in Ireland, "though the Bronx is crowded with Irishmen too, lad, not
just
Woodside." Some soccer buddies moseyed our way and slapped him
on the
back and said, "Fookin' Coshteleff," and made him laugh and left the
bar. He

shocked me when he asked if he could come back to my place. I
wouldn't
have guessed he was gay. I wouldn't have guessed he was bi. It was
thrilling to
think people thought he was straight because somewhere inside me
I'd always

wanted to sleep with my father. He was good at kissing, surprising at
kissing, a
father to kiss me, and extremely nice with his Irish lilt and lavish balls
and feet
hanging over the edge of my bed. I thought that, being so forward
and friendly

and eager to suck me, he'd want to be lovers. But he just wanted sex.
Well, that's
how I saw it. Though I knew I'd over-burdened him by calling him
three or
four days in a row, in the night and in the morning, like he'd stolen
my wallet.

Take That to the Bank

I dance out onto a crummy stage, thrilled by the notice of
all twelve customers, shedding my normally measly demeanor
as an urgent rhythmic guitar motif disinhibits my hips.

An audition took place a couple days earlier,
three whisky sours on an empty stomach,
as the regular dancers in chokers and Speedos
and shitkicker boots materialized from
the back somewhere and gathered up front
to applaud me and hoot like they
knew me already and steadied my knees.
The baggy-eyed Greek lady (she'd said to
me earlier, "Come. You oh-dition") cut into
the record and said I was hired.

Now I'm shy and conceited and strutting to an intricate new-wave
    beat and focused
on an unresisting smile in the middle of the crummy theater that
    looks up in wonder
as I wriggle out of skivvies—low-cut and shimmery—with a
    leprechaun logo—and
Marianne Faithful's Broken English dwindles away. ("What are you
    fighting for?")

The other dancers dance by turns (six of us
total) for an audience of hard-up joes,
after which a porno plays—JEREMIAH'S
JOHNSON or FIVE SLEAZY PIECES—
projected by the Greek lady as I meanwhile
slip into shorts, no shirt, and cat around
the lobby as all of us cat when our boogie
is through where the unresisting guy from
the middle of the theater with its broken

64

seats is smiling and waiting to shake my
hand. I usher him back to a black-walled
room after threading behind the black box
stage where assorted strippers are clothed
and stripped and the unresisting smiler
(no shoulders) (from Allentown, he says)
fondles my dick (it's one-third hard) and
giggles like a twelve-year-old—that's all he
wants—and pays me thirty-five dollars (cash).

The money'll help me restart my life—
that's the point of all this—
well one of the points—
what a pointless year since college—
but it hadn't occurred to me while running a finger down
the ads in the *Voice* that a job like this would advertise.

I get to know the other performers:

Winston Wilde in biker drag with his insolent gyrations.

Two Colombians from middle Queens (straight and cousins, believe
      it or not, Winston says)
with beautiful plump unwrinkled scrotums and rice and beans in
      plastic containers.

A six-foot, three-inch Black flamingo (stage name Potpourri
      Sashay) who peels en pointe
   to *Planet Claire* and reads *No Exit* in the original French when he
      isn't glissading.

Street tough Manny, a.k.a. Scorch ("rebel rebel how could they
know"), stomping into the lights unconcerned about the beat.

I'm surprised they're all nice, even stuck-up Potpourri, and
      sometimes between

65

shows (seven a day) we crowd into Howard Johnson's with its
　　windows on
Broadway (clean gigantic spectacle windows) for pancakes and
　　banana splits.

Winston gets me to buy some boots—the kind the Texas tourists
wear—for sixty-nine dollars, right in Times Square, to butch up my
　　act.

And the customers, the tricks:

　　A construction worker (in Timberlands) from Bay Ridge (clearly
　　　　closeted)
　　who shows up twice (how flattering) and goes all the way (fifty
　　　　bucks double).

An eighty-year-old from rural Maine with a muskrat wig and a young
　　man's choppers
who pays me a hundred in travelers checks to sleep with him at the
　　Chelsea Hotel.

　　A brassy hairy big-bellied Hawaiian ensconced at the Algonquin
　　in possession of a bamboo bong and suspicious gold doubloons.

A bear with a beard from West 96th Street (he takes me there in
a bumblebee cab) who breaks his own bed in the middle of the job.

　　And a—what have we here? Five-o'clock
　　stubble on the face of a handsome nine-
　　o'clock rabbi with a Talmud crammed in
　　an open-top briefcase. (I've ushered him back
　　to the black-walled room.) "That's Buvva Metzia,"
　　I tell him, stunned, reading the spine
　　(בּ אבָ מְ עיצ). He says, "How do you know
　　that?" "I went to yeshiva. We studied
　　that tract!" He recreates a Talmud class

with minimal furniture—table and chair
—and I read aloud from his jumbo book
the law about a wine barrel blown off
a roof that kills someone's ox in bygone
Babylonia while the teacher just happens
to paw the pupil (I have never in my life
been as horny as this) dressed in a
yellowing tzitzis poncho the rabbi provides
and the Texas boots and nothing else.

I get to San Francisco on the money I make—three thousand
    dollars—
a fortune back then—after eleven days of AP Erotic
Economics. And the clout I command at the edge of the stage
charts a through line of resourceful peacocking recklessness
(alluded to in a Yom Kippur prayer about the sins you commit
"in a gathering of lewdness") that never lets me down.

Liz Kingsley

Triple Sonnet for What I Want

I want my wife to love it when I crack
    my knuckles and share what my students had the gall
to say, to think I'm hysterical, sexy, clever
    even in my toothpaste-stained Uggs. I want her
to turn off the Tarheels, turn and face me.
    Put away the crosswords, Sudoku, Spelling Bee.
I want her to start drinking again so
    I can resume it too, for us to sit
in our swivel chairs clinking our wedding
    Waterford, toasting each other, sipping vodka
as we slip into silliness, maybe
    spill which stay-at-home mom we've had our eye on.
I'm antsy, horny, hungry, oh lord her
    slender fingers, but that's not all I want—

I want her to look at me, look me dead
    (though that sounds dramatic) in my green eyes
with the golden rings, in my one gray-tinged
    eyebrow, in my taut calves, in my sweet ass
(her words, not mine!) and see what she used to,
    what made her interrupt her own thoughts—
how irresistible, how made for her—
    and pull me close no matter who's around.
I still have those parts and I've got new ones
    too, like more distinguished Salt-n-Pepa
hair. She could say, "You make me wanna shoop,
    Shoop-a-doop, shoop-a-doop-a-doop-a-doop,"
like she once did. I want her jaw to drop,
    maybe drool a little when I walk by.

Greed isn't so bad, it looks ravishing
     on me. I want even more. So, she's found
her inner peace with morning pages, tea,
     yoga, HIIT rides on the bike, "Connections,"
all of which is great. She even meditates.
     I'm grateful she's come to appreciate
the solitude that I have always craved
     And yet I fear that she's fallen too hard
for herself and all that she's discovered.
     I get it; I fell hard for her as well.
Her burgeoning enlightenment is hot.
     I want her to be self-possessed, knowing
just what she needs, but not at the expense
     of me. Of me, damnit, of me, me, me!

In Memoriam: Late 1970s - 2023

I pay tribute to my clitoral orgasm for her contribution to my overall happiness. Born circa 1979 in the basement of 52 Ross Hall while I straddled the thin wall of a plastic toy box, her arrival was a surprise. She visited me steadily, in rapid succession, for forty-four years. Her twin, my vaginal orgasm, tragically died at birth, leaving the burden of my satisfaction squarely on her shoulders. May they be reunited in lasting peace. Her demise was unexpected; she was vivacious until the very end. I thought that menopause, wreaking such wide-ranging havoc, might have made her shy around my wife. I tried reviving her myself, to no avail. She loved life, displaying her talents in homes, cars, hotels, bodies of water, movie theaters, public buses, and in one particularly memorable moment, the bathroom in the dean's office of a public university. There is solace in knowing she reached her peace before declining into atrophy. She is survived by lifelong erogenous partners: my nipples, anus, and the backs of my knees, and is already sorely, sorely missed. Burial will be private. In lieu of flowers, donations to the North American Menopause Society (NAMS) are appreciated.

Letter from My Vagina to the KY Jelly in My Wife's Drawer

I'm writing to apologize. Look, I'm not without manners; I know the proper way to greet someone. It's just that while you introduce yourself as a friend, I see mockery in your soothing blue packaging and the giant scripted "glide" across your tube. You advertise yourself without shame (I guess the shame is all mine). You're here to help. I get that. Gretchan has been trying to work you into our bed for a while, and she doesn't invite easily. Try to understand where I'm coming from. Close your eyes and imagine a vagina with a pleasing disposition and a sly sense of humor. A jackpot. A player. That's what I've always been, ready to go with a moment's notice. And then, a couple of years sneak by, I'm in my 50s, and I can't quite hang. It's not that I don't want to—I have a hard time rallying. "It's okay, sweet, dried raisin," I tell myself. I know, I know, I'm not the first. It's the natural course of things. You don't have to lecture me. I'm no longer an instrument of production or reproduction. And, of course, you know all this because, as you smugly boast, you've been around "Since 1904." I realize I'm taking my frustration out on you, which isn't quite fair, and I am sorry. I just find you a little brazen and cold to the touch, though you manage not to smell, and as much as I hate to admit it, you get the job done. I hope we can find a way. How can I put it? It's a little like greeting the funeral director with a huge smile and asking how his day is going.

71

Rapture

This morning, my eight-year-old
student who'd normally rather eat
nails than put his thoughts on paper,
agreed to respond to a prompt
about what he'd buy if he had
all the money on Earth. A mansion,
of course, which he knew how
to spell. "It would have so many
things," he wrote, to which I,
of course, asked, "Like what?
Give me a peek inside."

He squealed, eyes open wide
as he described the worlds within,
his desire doing cartwheels. An inside
pool, a spa, a library, a movie theater,
a free candy shop, an inside garden,
a trampoline park, a hot tub, a Disney
cruise, a claw machine, a race track,
a science lab, an escape room,
an Olivia Rodrigo concert, a sauna,
the planet's biggest wine bottle, a zoo
with every beast, a time machine,
a restaurant that robots own, a rocket
park, penguins on a glacier, a hibachi
grill, toys that come alive, a green room,
a billion trillion dogs, and, and, and, and…
much to his chagrin, we ran out of time.

He imagined massively, wrote so much.
While he read it to me, I closed my eyes
and promised to glimpse his paradise,
but all I saw was you—your furniture, your
arcade, your internal animal preserve,
my desire doing handsprings of its own.

Amanda Bales

Orono

I.

Snow chalks the slate lake.
Only the ice moans.
The loons are longing elsewhere.

First, I thought sex a caution,
then a violence, then a chore—
then her, and I was opened.

Flat backed we floated
summer marsh dank wet.
She left when the loons left.

II.

Winter snaps. Some birds remain.
Crack their beaks on lichen rocks.
I peck her texts. These false greens.

III.

When I walk, the wind
erases my tracks and I
wonder if I have ever

left this house. But I must have.
There are things here I did not make:
footstool, electric cord, stationary.

I did make *a mess of things*,
according to my mother, which is
one way to think of it, I guess.

IV.

The tree above me forgot
to slough and iced leaves
rattle like split shot weights

I maracaed as a child.
I swung hips and hair
sidestepped the upset

of landed fish gasp.
Motions to mimic
the act I would learn

as pain, terror, mundane,
and finally love that left me
mouth gaped ashore,

unsure lungs pained full,
my nascent adaptive anatomy
not enough, turns out, for her.

V.

In her wake, I entreated flat rock
and club but got the boot flick
back to choppy waters:

a pointless amnesty.
A fish returned too suddenly
will shock and die.

VI.

Dad always said he'd rather
be lucky than good, a lesson
taught at the reel but spun

out to nest inside the rest
of my life. A good man,
he thought himself lucky

to land my mother but
if that was luck I'd hate
to see the loser and since

I know we share more
than vitiligo trout back hands—
Well, lucky her, to break free.

And lucky me. If luck
is what we're calling it.

Foley

the reproduction of everyday sounds added to media
a catheter held in place by a water-filled balloon

The sound your mother makes is *home*, so what choice? You take her. The sound your mother makes is *thank you*. Her clocks and crosses and dust-clumped ceiling fan. The sound your mother makes is *drink*, so straw pipettes down her swallow-slack throat. The sound your mother makes is *where* about people known, unknown; her own home; her own body. The sound your mother makes is moan when your idiot hands catch Foley on bed frame. The sound your mother makes is gurgle, her heart stuttering to tumored lungs. The sound your mother makes is no sound.

The Queer at the Baptist Funeral

In a state that wants me dead
In a town that wants me dead
In a church that wants me dead

I listen to men who want me dead
say prayers about my dead mother

I keep my eyes open

Ben Hellerstein

Long Point Light, Provincetown

Here is pulled taut the stuff of continents
anchored some sixty miles hence, here pegged,
here wound around the whitewashed lighthouse walls,
that squat square building midst the sandy scrub.

The tense cord shivers, and the landscape sings
in parabolic hills and backwashed coves;
we feel the over- and the under-tones,
a clamor of sympathetic harmonies
resonating in our vacant bodies,
calling us to clamber over sand dunes,
skip across the heaped-up granite boulders
and pitch ourselves against the lighthouse walls.

The beacon catches; if we make it turn,
perhaps we'll bring us closer into tune.

Narragansett, Rhode Island

Seaward sounds a gulls' chorus—who will heed
such senseless squawking? Whether a blessing
or burden, speech is our most hopeful summons:
Call me to the water, call me with words.

Your bay's an arm of the greater ocean;
they flow one into the other unbounded.
Will we learn something of a profound world
or hear little beyond the breakwater?
Will you and I speak sense or mumble surf?
Will we breathe freely or choke on salt fumes?
Will we comprehend or will we fall close,
trumpets silent in the depths unsounded?

If asked, I'll stand with you where the waves sweep
and wash, and let the sand swallow our feet.

From a watercolor painter to a writer

Bludgeon me with inky blots on bleached sheets
and I'll paint scattered leaves in purple-dun
and needle you evergreen; my sky will bleed
blue into pallid snow, your letters run,
figures befog, our wetted pigments puddle
on the ragged page, like dreams unread.
Of turbid characters we make a muddle.
Let's assume that in the year ahead
we find more artful and more subtle ways
to say the things we feel about each other:
We'll decipher in resplendent days
what to ourselves unconscious have discovered.
    Let's let dry, and sleep while it is dark,
    and in the morning make a cleaner mark.

Contributors

Amanda Bales is a queer writer and union activist living in central Illinois with her dog, Axton. She is a Teaching Assistant Professor at the University of Illinois, Urbana-Champaign and the author of *Pekolah Stories* (Cowboy Jamboree Press 2021). Her work has also appeared in *Southern Humanities Review*, *The Cincinnati Review* MiCro Series, *Raleigh Review*, and elsewhere.

Kit Evans is a queer poet and writer from Oregon. He is a current MFA student at Pacific University. His poetry has appeared in *The Dewdrop*, *Hiram Poetry Review*, *THRUSH*, *Vagabond City Lit*, and others. When not writing, Kit can often be found next to large bodies of water, or lifting rocks in search of cool bugs.

Ben Hellerstein lives in Indiana and is pursuing a PhD in environmental policy, studying the politics and policy of the transition to renewable energy. He was recently selected as a finalist in the *Atlanta Review*'s annual international poetry competition.

Ash Helms-Tippit writes fiction and poetry, while also studying children's literature, queer literature, animal studies, and intersectional feminism. Originally from Alabama, she is currently working on a Ph.D. in English/Creative Writing at the University of Louisiana, Lafayette.

Arumandhira Howard is a Blasian queer writer born and raised in Indonesia (now surviving in Los Angeles). She has received support from Kundiman and Storyknife Writers Retreat as a poetry fellow. Her works have appeared in *Honey Literary*, *The Boiler*, *The Offing*, the Asian American Writers' Workshop magazine, *Split This Rock*, *BRUISER Mag*, and *SWWIM*.

Lauren Howton (she/her) earned a Ph.D. from Florida State University and an MFA from McNeese State University. She previously served as a poetry editor for the *Southeast Review* and Managing Editor for the *McNeese Review*. She currently lives in Auburn, Alabama, with her corgi, Norman, and teaches at Auburn University.

Liz Kingsley's poems appear in *New Ohio Review*, *The Round*, *The McNeese Review*, *Cagibi*, *Euphony Journal*, *Sweet: A Literary Confection*, and other magazines. Her fiction has appeared in *The William and Mary Review*, and her essays have been published in *New Jersey Family Magazine* and the anthology *Blended: Writers on the Stepfamily Experience*. She is an MFA candidate at the Rainier Writing Workshop at Pacific Lutheran University. When not writing, she works as an elementary special education teacher. Liz lives in New Jersey with her wife, some of their grown children, and various animals. Her poems live at lizkingsleywriter.com.

Joshua Kulseth earned his B.A. in English from Clemson University, his M.F.A. in poetry from Hunter College, and his Ph.D. in poetry from Texas Tech University. His poems have appeared and are forthcoming in *Tar River Poetry*, *The Emerson Review*, *The Potomac Review*, *The Windhover*, *The South Carolina Review* and others. His poetry manuscript, *Leaving Troy*, was shortlisted for the *Cider Press Review* Publication Competition, and is currently under contract with Finishing Line Press.

Daniel W.K. Lee (李華強) is a third-generation refugee, queer, Cantonese American born in Kuching, Malaysia. He earned his Master of Fine Arts in Creative Writing at The New School, and his debut collection of poetry, *Anatomy of Want*, was published by QueerMojo/ Rebel Satori Press. Daniel lives in New Orleans with his head-turning whippet Camden. Find out more about him at danielwklee.com, join his Patreon at patreon.com/danielwklee, or follow him: @strongplum on Instagram.

Daniel Meltz was raised in the low-rent reaches of New Jersey, sixteen minutes from Times Square, and has lived in Manhattan for fifty years. He's a retired technical writer and teacher of Deaf young people, with a B.A. from Columbia (no honors). Both his first book of poems, *It Wasn't Easy to Reach You*, from Trail to Table, and his first novel, *Rabbis of the Garden State*, from Rattling Good Yarns, have been published just minutes ago in 2025.

Bleah Patterson is a queer, Southern poet born and raised in Texas. She has been a Pushcart Prize and Best of Net nominee. Much of her work explores the contention between identity and home and has been featured or is forthcoming in various journals, including *Electric Literature, Pinch, Write or Die, The Laurel Review, Phoebe Literature*, and *Taco Bell Quarterly*.

Jendi Reiter is the author of five poetry books and chapbooks, most recently *Made Man* (Little Red Tree, 2022); the story collection *An Incomplete List of My Wishes* (Sunshot Press/New Millennium Writings, 2018); and the novels *Origin Story* (Saddle Road Press, 2024) and *Two Natures* (Saddle Road Press, 2016). *Origin Story* was a finalist for the Big Moose Prize from Black Lawrence Press, and *Two Natures* won the Rainbow Award for Best Gay Contemporary Fiction. They are the editor of the writing resource site WinningWriters.com.

Branwell Roberts (he/they) is a British poet living in Australia. Their work uses classical and historical themes to explore queer gender(s) and sexuality from a trans perspective. Branwell graduated from the MFA program at Manchester Writing School and is currently working on a Ph.D. at the University of Tasmania, writing poetry about the history of Antarctic exploration. Branwell can be found on Twitter (@ branwellroberts) and Bluesky (branwellroberts.bsky.social).

Mandy Shunnarah (they/them) is an Alabama-born Appalachian and Palestinian-American writer in Columbus, Ohio. Their essays, poetry, and short stories have been published in *The New York Times*, *Electric Literature*, *The Rumpus*, and others. They won the *Porter House Review* 2024 Editor's Prize in Poetry and are supported by the Ohio Arts Council, Greater Columbus Arts Council, and Sundress Academy for the Arts. Their first book, *Midwest Shreds: Skating Through America's Heartland*, was released in 2024 from Belt Publishing, and their second book, a poetry collection titled *We Had Mansions*, is forthcoming from Diode Editions in 2025. Read more at mandyshunnarah.com.

Victoria Sosa is a poet, author, and screenwriter from Lake Charles, Louisiana, currently based in New Orleans. She holds a B.A. in English Writing from Loyola University New Orleans. Her work, which explores themes of loss, transformation, and healing from a queer feminist perspective, has recently garnered recognition. She was a finalist in the Del Shores 2024 Writers Search and the 2024 *Kinsman Quarterly* Iridescence Award.

Our Finalist Judge

Nikki Ummel has been published by *The Georgia Review, Black Lawrence Press*, and others. She is the 2022 recipient of the Leslie McGrath Poetry Prize and 2023 recipient of the Juxtaprose Poetry Award for her manuscript, *Bloom*. Nikki is the co-founder of LMNL, an arts organization focused on readings, workshops, and residencies. She has two poetry chapbooks, *Hush* (Belle Point Press, 2022) and *Bayou Sonata* (NOLA DNA, 2023), funded by the New Orleans Jazz and Heritage Foundation.

About Our Editors

Jan Edwards Hemming's poetry and essays have appeared in *Electric Literature*, *McSweeney's Internet Tendency*, *Los Angeles Review of Books Blog*, *The Ilanot Review*, *FruitSlice*, and elsewhere. Her poems "Bird" and "Oven" were each nominated for a Pushcart Prize, and her essay "Mirror, Mirror" was nominated for the Best American Essays 2025. She holds an MFA in Poetry from NYU and a B.A. in English from LSU, has been awarded residencies from Virginia Center for Creative Arts and Vermont Studio Center, and co-edited the 2023 and 2024 Saints+Sinners Literary Festival Poetry Anthologies. She lives and works in New Orleans.

Paul J. Willis, Executive Director/Project Director, has over 29 years of experience in nonprofit management. He earned a B.S. in Psychology and an M.S. in Communication. He started his administrative work in 1992 as the co-director of the Holos Foundation in Minneapolis. The Foundation operated an alternative high school program for at-risk youth. Willis has been the executive director of the Tennessee Williams & New Orleans Literary Festival since 2004. He is the founder of the Saints+Sinners Literary Festival (established in 2003), and has edited various anthologies, including the most recent *Saints+Sinners: New Fiction from the Festival 2025*. He was the 2019 recipient of the Publishing Triangle Leadership Award for contributions to the LGBTQ+ literary community.

About Our Cover Artist

Timothy Cummings, represented by Catharine Clark Gallery in San Francisco and Nancy Hoffman Gallery in New York, journeyed to a French Quarter pied-à-terre overlooking Armstrong Park in the Fall of 2017 as part of a My Good Judy Residency. The My Good Judy Foundation provides residencies for artists seeking to produce a body of work or performance in New Orleans that address culture making from an LGBTQ perspective. The residency was established to also honor the work of author and activist Judy Grahn. The subjects of Cummings' work are often children and adolescents struggling with issues of sexuality and sexual orientation in an adult world. In 2013, he was an artist-in-residence and subject of a solo exhibition at Transarte in Sao Paulo, Brazil. His paintings are also part of the collections of singer, songwriter, and composer, Rufus Wainwright, Whoopi Goldberg in Los Angeles, CA, and Tomaso Bracco, and Sara Davis in Milan, Italy. Timothy enjoyed his time in New Orleans, where he received inspiration from the spirits of his favorite writers, Tennessee Williams and Truman Capote. "They shaped my early adolescence. They offer a magical telling of the spirit of this place. The darkness and humor of life and the queer Southern aesthetic shows up in my work as well. Williams' 'garrulous grotesques', replacing the bleak mundane of the world with a lush queer poetic eye for the shadows is part of my focus," Cummings said. He graciously created an original painting of Tennessee Williams to be used as the cover art for the COVID-cancelled 2020 Tennessee Williams & New Orleans Literary Festival. For the 20th Anniversary of Saints+Sinners, Timothy created the original painting, *Incident at the Carousel Bar*, featuring a young Tennessee Williams and a mysterious masked companion. We are so proud to use his artwork on our Festival program book covers, and we thank Timothy for the generous donation of his paintings to the Festival's fundraising efforts. He resides in a tiny house in Albuquerque, New Mexico. You can see more of Timothy's work at: www.cclarkgallery.com/artists/series/timothy-cummings and at www. nancyhoffmangallery.com/artist-timothy-cummings

Saints+Sinners Literary Festival

The first **Saints+Sinners Literary Festival** took place in May of 2003. The event started as a new initiative designed as an innovative way to reach the community with information about HIV/AIDS. It was also formed to bring the LGBTQ+ community together to celebrate the literary arts. Literature has long nurtured hope and inspiration, and has provided an avenue of understanding. A steady stream of LGBTQ+ novels, short stories, poems, plays, and nonfiction works has served to awaken lesbians, gay men, bisexuals, and transgendered persons to the existence of others like them; to trace the outlines of a shared culture; and to bring the outside world into the emotional passages of LGBTQ+ life.

After the Stonewall Riots in New York City, gay literature finally came "out of the closet." In time, noted authors, such as Dorothy Allison, Michael Cunningham, and Mark Doty (all past Saints' participants), were receiving mainstream award recognition for their works. But there are still few opportunities for media attention of gay-themed books, and decreasing publishing options. This Festival helps to ensure that written work from the LGBTQ+ community will continue to have an outlet, and that people will have access to books that will help dispel stereotypes, alleviate isolation, and provide resources for personal wellness.

The event has since evolved into a program of the Tennessee Williams & New Orleans Literary Festival made possible by our premier sponsor, the John Burton Harter Foundation. The Saints+Sinners LGBTQ+ Literary Festival works to achieve the following goals:

1. to create an environment for productive networking to ensure increased knowledge and dissemination of LGBTQ+ literature;
2. to provide an atmosphere for discussion, brainstorming, and the emergence of new ideas;

3. to recognize and honor writers, editors, and publishers who broke new ground and made it possible for LGBTQ+ books to reach an audience; and
4. to provide a forum for authors, editors, and publishers to talk about their work for the benefit of emerging writers, and for the enjoyment of readers of LGBTQ+ literature.

Saints+Sinners is an annual celebration that takes place in the heart of the French Quarter of New Orleans each spring. The Festival includes writing workshops, readings, panel discussions, literary walking tours, and a variety of special events. We also aim to inspire the written word through our short fiction contest, and our annual Saints+Sinners Emerging Writer Award sponsored by Rob Byrnes. Each year we induct individuals to our Saints+Sinners Hall of Fame. The Hall of Fame is intended to recognize people for their dedication to LGBTQ+ literature. Selected members have shown their passion for our literary community through various avenues including writing, promotion, publishing, editing, teaching, bookselling, and volunteerism.

Past year's inductees into the Saints+Sinners Literary Hall of Fame include: Dorothy Allison, Carol Anshaw, Ann Bannon, Samiya Bashir, Nancy K Bereano, David Bergman, Lucy Jane Bledsoe, Maureen Brady, Jericho Brown, Rob Byrnes, Patrick Califia, Louis Flint Ceci, Bernard Cooper, Timothy Cummings, Michael Cunningham, Jameson Currier, Brenda Currin, Mark Doty, Mark Drake, Jim Duggins, Elana Dykewomon, Amie M. Evans, Otis Fennell, Michael Thomas Ford, Katherine V. Forrest, Nancy Garden, Mary Gauthier, Lawrence Henry Gobble, Jewelle Gomez, Judy Grahn, Jim Grimsley, David Groff, Tara Hardy, Ellen Hart, Charyl Head, Greg Herren, Kenneth Holditch, Andrew Holleran, Candice Huber, Fay Jacobs, G. Winston James, Saeed Jones, Raphael Kadushin, Michele Karlsberg, Judith Katz, Moises Kaufman, Irena Klepfisz, Joan Larkin, Susan Larson, Lee Lynch, Jeff Mann, William J. Mann, Marianne K. Martin, Paula Martinac, Stephen McCauley, Val McDermid, Mark Merlis, Tim Miller, Kay Murphy, Rip & Marsha Naquin-Delain, Michael Nava, Achy Obejas, Frank Perez, Felice Picano, Radclyffe, J.M. Redmann, Lance Ringel, David Rosen, Carol Rosenfeld, Steven Saylor, Carol

Seajay, Martin Sherman, Kelly Smith, William Christy Smith, Pamela Sneed, Jack Sullivan, Carsen Taite, Cecilia Tan, Justin Torres, Noel Twilbeck, Jr., Patricia Nell Warren, Don Weise, Jess Wells, Edmund White, Paul J. Willis, and Emanuel Xavier.

For more information about the Saints+Sinners Archangel Membership Program, visit www.sasfest.org. Be sure to sign up for our e-newsletter for updates for future programs. We hope you will join other writers and bibliophiles for a weekend of literary revelry not to be missed!

"Saints+Sinners is hands down one of the best places to go to revive a writer's spirit. Imagine a gathering in which you can lean into conversations with some of the best writers and editors and agents in the country, all of them speaking frankly and passionately about the books, stories and people they love and hate and want most to record in some indelible way. Imagine a community that tells you truthfully what is happening with writing and publishing in the world you most want to reach. Imagine the flirting, the arguing, the teasing and praising and exchanging of not just vital information, but the whole spirit of queer arts and creating. Then imagine it all taking place on the sultry streets of New Orleans' French Quarter. That's Saints+Sinners—the best wellspring of inspiration and enthusiasm you are going to find. Go there."

—**Dorothy Allison**, National Book Award finalist for *Bastard Out of Carolina*, and author of the critically acclaimed novel *Cavedweller*.